EVERYONE SHOULD PLAY GOLF

Marilyn Merrifield

Copyright © 2020 Marilyn Merrifield

All rights reserved.
ISBN: 9798629650508
Imprint: Independently published

No part of this book may be reproduced, or stored in a retrieval system, or transmitted in any form or by any means, electronic, mechanical, photocopying, recording, or otherwise, without express written permission of the publisher.

Dedicated to my wonderful husband Rich who demonstrated great wisdom and restraint in never coaching but always encouraging me. To my golf gals Carolyn thank you for being my partner for all these years. Joanne, you always inspire me to improve. Thank you also to everyone in the golf league who have allowed me to play and grow.

Lastly, I especially want to dedicate this book to my children and encourage all four to get their hole in ones.

EVERYONE SHOULD PLAY GOLF

by
Marilyn Merrifield

Table Of Contents

EVERYONE SHOULD PLAY GOLF
  by
  Marilyn Merrifield

INTRODUCTION

HOLE 1 – PAR 4 -QUIET THE MIND

HOLE 2 – PAR 4 – ENGAGE IN POSITIVE SELF TALK

HOLE 3 - PAR 3 LESSON 3 – SHOOT FOR THE MOON!

HOLE 4 – PAR 5 –GOLF LIES?

HOLE 5 – CHANGE IS HARD

HOLE 6 – PAR 4 MANAGING YOUR MISSES

HOLE 7 - TIME MANAGEMENT

HOLE 8 -PAR 5 -KINDNESS

HOLE 9 – PAR 4 – IF YOU CAN'T LAUGH AT YOURSELF – OTHERS WILL

HOLE 10 – RESILLANCE

HOLE 11 – BETTER TO LOSE YOUR BALL THAN YOUR TEMPER

HOLE 12 – DON'T BE AN A**HOLE

HOLE 13 – IT'S ELEMENTAL

HOLE 14 – FOR THE LADIES

HOLE 15 – AGING AND LIMITATIONS

HOLE 16 – PARENTING

HOLE 17 – WILD WILDLIFE

HOLE 18 – GRATITUDE

THE 19TH HOLE – CAMARADERIE

❖ ❖ ❖

Introduction

You should know right at the start, that I am not very good at golf.
WAIT, keep reading!
If you're are looking for a book about how to improve your putting, or get more distance off the tee, this is not that book.
WAIT, keep reading!
Look, there are a ton of books written by people that aim to teach you how to play. What I want to share with you is **WHY** you should play. I hope to convince you that playing golf will:

- Help you in other aspects of your life
- Help you discover things about yourself
- Be a lifelong game to play with family and friends

I hope you will come to love the game as much as I do and to realize that golf will lead you down a road of self-discovery and personal growth. Whether you are contemplating taking up golf, or have been playing for many years, it is my hope that you will find in these short pages, a new way of thinking about this game, and come to see that it's not just another game.

People talk about finding themselves or discovering "who they are" all the time. Guess what? You can cut out a lot of time sitting around meditating and just play golf. If you pay attention, you will learn more about yourself than you could have imagined. This game is a microcosm of life. The values you profess and aspire to are brought into sharp focus in the mirror of your actions. It is a gift to gain so much insight.

Now, some people say, golf builds character, but that doesn't sound like fun to me. Boot camp builds character and that doesn't sound like any fun whatsoever to all but a select few masochists. Golf IS after all a game, and it's a lot of fun. Unlike other games in which you run around and move quickly, when you play golf you have time to think, to take in the surroundings, to be with friends or get to know new people and experience joy.

After reading this book, you will have a better sense of what to look for in your journey to know yourself and others better. You will see qualities and virtues in your friends that will help your relationship grow. Whether you are just thinking of starting or you're a seasoned golfer, it is my hope that you will see golf in a new way.

You and I will play a round of golf. Just us, on this beautiful tree lined golf course. Let's see how each hole unfolds. The greens are perfect, there's no one behind us, it is a gorgeous day in the high 70's, the grass glistens from the early morning dew which will soon give way to a bright and sunny day. All is right with the world. Join me on the first tee.

❖ ❖ ❖

Hole 1 - Quiet The Mind

Here we are, I'm so excited to be out here, I've looked forward to this round all week, and to spending time with you. Golf is a social game, it's a great way to have fun and relax while you get to know the people you're playing with or you catch up with friends and family or meet new people. Unlike a sport like tennis, there is opportunity in golf to chat and to commiserate over a bad lie, applaud a great shot or strategize on your approach.

I won't lie to you, for most people the first hole is the hardest hole – why? There's usually a few people watching - the rest of your group, the starter (the person who tells you when it is your turn to go) and sometimes the next group waiting for their turn. It always feels like everyone is watching you and well… they are!

You want to hit a good drive off the tee.

You want to show off your hard work on the driving range.

You don't want to suck.

You get up there, put the tee in the grass then the brain starts going – "did I tee it too high, what if I whiff the ball, I didn't have time to hit a warm up bucket". Some people actually start vocalizing this negative self-talk – it sounds like this: "I haven't been out much this year", or This is the first time I've swung a club in a month".

STOPPPPP

This is a great opportunity to stop the brain, check in with yourself and quiet your mind. The ability to be center yourself and focus is a life skill. I'm not talking about sitting in a lotus position for an hour - but seriously can you tune everything and everyone out of your mind for 10 – 30 seconds?

Our lives have become so busy, there's so much to do and not enough time to do it. We run from activity to activity. The demands on our lives are intense and our thoughts seem to be constantly focused on what we need to do next. Our brains are flooded with worries, stress, chores and tasks. Our cell phones seem to never stop and these days, employers seem to expect that our time away from the office is just a change in our work venue. Far too often, the expectation is that we will complete work afterhours. We desperately need to reclaim our leisure time, if only so that we can be more present to our families. But what about us? Don't we need some real down time to decompress.

So, today, I bring with me to this tee box, the anxieties of the week from work, home, school, chores that are not done. They are not gone from my life but I cannot attend to those right now. I'm here right now. **Here.** Not there. I turn off the phone because it is not o.k. to use your phone on the course. You and I have the opportunity to give our racing brain a rest for a few hours and experience joy and freedom from all the anxiety that may be part of your hustle bustle life and give your brain a rest.

Give yourself the gift of taking a moment to look out toward the faraway flag, take a deep breath and shrug your shoulders. Take a practice swing and let her rip. Listen for the "Whack", and watch your ball sail gracefully onto the fairway. Listen as the rest of the foursome exclaims, "Nice shot" and smile. ☺

❖ ❖ ❖

Hole 2 - Positive Self Talk

Do you know someone who puts themselves down? They tell themselves that they are just not able to do something well? They aren't good at math, they can't present ideas well in work, they can't write a novel, they can't do x, they're not good at y, and they will never be able to z. Maybe it's true, maybe they aren't able to do those things but sometimes it's just a perception. It's not based on fact but rather, it is the "story" the person is telling him or herself. This type of thinking is self-limiting.

Many years ago, I learned a lesson from an elderly neighbor. My fence backed up to his. At the time, I was a young mother and wife. I came to loathe seeing this delightful man because he would always tell me things like "you know, my wife is the best cook in the world", "my wife is the best decorator I know", "my wife was the best mother in the world". Needless to say, I came to feel inferior to this mother, wife goddess next door as I compared my daily failures with my neighbor's compliments about his wife. One day I asked him, "you know Mr. Jones, you always have such high praise for your wife". A slow smile came over his face and he said, "you know, Marilyn, I learned early in my marriage something very important that has served our family very well. I learned that if you tell a lie often enough, it becomes real." My mouth dropped and we both laughed and laughed. What this very nice man meant was that giving his wife and kids positive messages made it more likely that they would live into the image that he had for them. What a concept!

Have you noticed that what you believe tends to come true? If you tell yourself you aren't good at physics, you probably won't be. If you tell yourself a story that you can't putt well, it is more likely that won't putt well. Focus on the one thing that you did right. I was happy with my fairway shot on the last hole. Last week I mostly one putted. If you are like me, from time to time you will get down on yourself, that's normal but try to recognize negative self talk and replace it with someting positive. You don't have to become an ego-maniac but you also don't need to put yourself down. Tell yourself things like:

- There is nothing that I can't do, with practice!
- I'm pretty confident that I can achieve most things that I choose to, I can point to other experiences in my life where I've mastered a new skill. I'm working on this one.
- I often one putt.

Like my former neighbor, it might be a lie that happily will come to be true...

❖ ❖ ❖

Hole 3 -Shoot For The Moon!

"Shoot for the moon. Even if you miss, you'll land among the stars."

— **Norman Vincent Peale**

Walk into any golf club and you will see a display on the wall that will list all the names of the people who have managed to get what can only be considered a golf miracle – a Hole in One. I bet you have walked by it without taking much notice. I love to see it and to see the names listed. There is a story behind each and every one. It is a reminder that miracles happen to ordinary people and at unexpected times. One day it will happen to me.

The National Hole In One Registry states that the average course has about 25,000 to 30,000 rounds played on it each year. Each course reports 10-15 holes in one each year. They place the odds of making a hole in one at 1:3500. Sounds tough, right? Not really if you think about it this way. About 15 people will get a hole in one on the course we are playing today this year, and it can be anybody – really anybody. I know what you're thinking, but read on dear friend.

It's going to happen on a Par 3, unless you are Superman. So, here's our chance we are on our first 3 today. Let's get a hole in one. NOT let's **try** to get a hole in one. Let's get a hole in one! Say it and mean it. When I say this out loud during a round, (as I frequently do) most people laugh at me. Why do they laugh? It can happen and it does happen. Why can't it happen now? Why not you, why not me?

If you reach for the moon and don't make it what is the worst that will happen? You will have given it a shot. You tried. Why not approach this hole with the attitude that you will make it and maybe you'll get a bogie or a par?

Perhaps because I come from extraordinarily modest means I have been fortunate to have trained myself to reach for things that might have seemed impossible – because really and truly all of it was "impossible". Yet somehow, most of those goals that I've set for myself have been obtained through luck, perseverance and hard work, or the grace of God – likely all of the above. I don't really know.

But what I do know is that:
- A hole in one is scored once in 3,500 rounds
- It is not impossible or no one would do it
- 16% of holes in ones are made by women
- Most holes in ones will not be obtained by pros and;
- 60% are golfers who are over 50.
- It could be me, or YOU – right here, right now

For the doubters out there, let me share with you this true story. Week after week during the summer of 2018, my golf partner in a co-ed company league heard me share with our opponents exactly what I've written here. Every single Wednesday we played a different twosome. As we approached this very same Par 3, I would explain to them that we should get a hole in one, how it was nuts that no one in our league had gotten a hole in one and my sentiment that we just weren't trying hard enough. I honestly didn't care who got the hole in one just that someone in our league should since we were by my reckoning overdue.

After the third week of hearing my little pep talk, my partner Carolyn (her real name) who by day is a statistician started rolling her eyes and as the year progressed, I think that her displeasure increased to outright hostility not aimed at me but at my "motivational" efforts. Week after week she encouraged me to give up on the hole in one litany - "Will you stop saying this", she would ask me. I would smile and say "Not until someone gets a hole in one".

Interestingly, some people would laugh at the idea or show some sort of amusement. But more than half the people thought about it and accepted that it WAS possible and went to the tee box with that thought in mind. Nearly everyone came much closer to the pin than they would have. That was a success in my mind because they acknowledged verbally, that having this thought had helped, which totally irritated Carolyn – which I confess, had now become part of my goal.

I had just finished writing the last chapter of this book when it was time for the end of the season league scramble. Our league's tradition is to have a season end scramble event followed by dinner. I wasn't paired with Carolyn that afternoon.

Imagine my surprise when my foursome finished and I dug out my phone to find a text from Carolyn and a triumphant picture of her and her hole in one. What irony, that the statistician and the naysayer got the hole in one! HA! So much for the odds. I take full credit for her hole in one. She says she got it so that I would shut up about this but now, the goal is for two holes in one next year.

I inquired at the pro shop if Carolyn's was the only one for 2018. The man at the shop smiled and said the incredible had happened.... "just last week, we had a guy who is 92 got his first hole in one AND a lady this week who is early 80's also got one using her driver. I rest my case – fairy tales can come true, they can happen to you – at any age!

I going to get one today... ☺
P.S. If you get one because of this book, you of course will write and tell me so we can discuss over the traditional drink you owe me and everyone in the clubhouse.

❖ ❖ ❖

Hole 4 – Golf Lies?

You need to get the little ball into the cup hitting it as few times as possible. That's really all you need to do. Simple, right? HA! All games have rules and for such a relatively simple game, golf has a ton of rules. I recently had the good fortune to meet a person who works on the updating of the US Golf Association Rule book. This gentleman was part of a group that was having lunch with a PGA professional after a lesson. Somehow, our lunch became a sort of quiz on the rules and it became evident that the rules are so obscure that mere mortals would be hard pressed to know all the nuances – this man even tripped our pro! It's a good idea to read through the rule book so you are familiar with the rules, but unless you're going to play in a tournament, you are good with a just a working knowledge of the game.

However, there is one very special rule that every player must know, one special fundamental rule that all other rules are based on which is that golf is dependent personal honesty and integrity. We are on the honor system. Players sign the scorecard attesting to their score and their good word is accepted. That is the spirit and soul of the game. These are pretty big words, Integrity, Honor, Honesty. Sometimes, I look at the news and see those hallmarks of good character are sadly in short supply.

Everyone I know, me included, would say that we are honest and would never cheat. But how often are we tested? Golf is like a gym workout for your honesty muscle. A great example of this is Brian Davis who was trying to win his first PGA Tour victory against Jim Fuyrk in 2010. Brian's ball landed in the bunker, there were some reeds around his ball. The rule is that you cannot hit anything but the ball. Brian hit the ball out of the bunker but wasn't sure if his club had touched a reed on the downswing. The referee did not call it, but Brian himself called him over and asked that they review the film to be sure. The film showed that the blade of grass did move and this cost Brian a two-stroke penalty and his first PGA Tour win. No one caught it but him. As I write this Brian still has not won a PGA Tour Victory, so the price he paid that day was great. Again, no one saw it but him. He could have just not said anything. What he says is that he could not have done otherwise and been true to himself. Golf is based on the integrity of the player and this is what makes golf great – and what makes Brian great.

We will never be in Brian's shoes, but in our own everyday lives we do get the opportunity to demonstrate to ourselves the same valor that Brian did. We can have those moments in which we show to ourselves that who we say we are is true. As an example, I play golf with a wonderful friend who I credit with teaching me many of the lessons here. When Joanne (her real name) hits an uncharacteristically terrible tee shot and all of us encourage her to take a mulligan (a do over) she won't do it. Why not? Because she reasons she would only be fooling herself. She plays it as it lies. I've learned a lot from Joanne over the years but this lesson, this True Golf Lesson has been invaluable and a testament to who she is.

There are some people who do things like never put down more than a triple bogey (3 more than par) on a hole, or will ground their ball in a bunker, or improve their lies or they have "breakfast balls". That's between them and their foursome. But ultimately, it comes down to you and your good name.

These lessons are so great for kids to learn and why golf is so great for young (and old). Now, before you feel too sorry for Brian Davis, you should know that he has earned over $13 Million dollars playing golf. So perhaps the golf gods have rewarded him in other ways, and you might be rewarded as well with the high esteem of your friends, and really that is priceless.

Hole 5 – Change Is Hard

There are things that we do that we don't even think about. Some are good habits and some are not so much. I brush and floss every day – good habit. I have a daily bedtime snack – not such a good habit. It's somewhat automatic. When we were little, our parents reminded us over and over again to do certain things until it was engraved in our brains. We heard it and heard it until we didn't even think about it anymore. When we learned how to drive a car, we thought about every little thing until it became somewhat automatic.

Athletes talk about "muscle memory". Sometimes I think I have muscle amnesia. I go through a setup routine each time which helps me "remember" what to do. Most people have a setup routine. Some golfers look at their target and give their club a waggle or tug at their shirt sleeve or touch their cap before a putt. Watch the pros on tv and see if you can identify what their routine is. The idea is that it becomes automatic and consistent.

There's a whole lot of stuff to pay attention to in golf, where your feet are in relation to the ball. Bending your knees, but not too much. Making sure to swing through the ball. Keep your head straight, have a flat back. It goes on and on. These are habits that become ingrained in us and we do it over and over again.

You might find that you can only progress only so far and that you might need to change something in order to continue to improve. My husband was doing o.k. but wasn't going to improve any further without an intervention by a golf pro. Golfers say they don't want to make a change in their swing because it will throw off their entire game until they get used to the change. That's often the case but what's the alternative – stay at the level you are at?

Change is hard – in life and in golf. In order to grow and improve, you need to go through that tough period of learning a new way of doing things and stumbling around a bit while you master the thing. It's that way with a job. You can stay in the same role, the same company doing the same thing but you won't progress in your career unless you're willing to change. And it might mean taking a step back so you can go two forward. Maybe in order to fix a draw, you might have to change your set up routine and suffer through the time it will take for the change to become automatic.

Change is hard, sometimes you have to leave something behind in order to improve with the full knowledge that it may not be better in the short term. I felt that way when I decided to change my putter. I was used to my putter, I feared that getting a new putter would take time to get used to. What would happen if it was actually worse than what I had now? But I was three putting and not improving. I had to try something different. Isn't that the way we sometimes feel when we are faced with a life change, a new job, a move to another city, for example? There is uncertainty and fear, we know that that there will be a period of adjustment and it will probably be somewhat painful, but we just aren't going to progress without fully committing to the change and following through. Commit and follow through with your shot and with life and it will work out.

❖ ❖ ❖

Hole 6 – Managing Your Misses

Sometimes when there are no good choices - only the best of two evils. You've been dealt a bad hand. You weigh your options, if I do X then this or that might happen, if I do Y then this other thing might happen. You agonize and agonize and then you make a choice, grit your teeth and go for it because you have to make a decision.

Today, the ball landed in the rough behind a tree. There's a chance that you can go between the trees and land on the green or you can chip it out and then go for the green. You think, no guts no glory – go for the green. Oh wait, there are bunkers on either side and if you go long, you land in a water hazard. Hmmm. Now what? How do you feel about taking the safe shot, do you feel like a loser if you play it safe, or do you feel superior because you managed to tame your ego?

Here's the thing, every time you are faced with a decision like this is different. That day is different, the way you feel is different, your level of confidence is different, etc. In general, when faced with no good options, you should typically manage your misses and take the safer option. For Pete's sake, don't make things worse. Don't land in the pond and have to take a penalty shot. Your ego (sometimes disguised as confidence) tells you can make it (maybe you can), like so many experiences, it is a choice and it is risk management.

The ego is very present on the golf course, you can see it in the people who play from the tips (furthest tee position) when they shouldn't. It's o.k. we are all learning and making mistakes, that's life. Maybe they are challenging themselves or having a bad day. No judgement, just an observation. Tell your ego to settle down and make sure to check in periodically to determine if you're demonstrating self-confidence or just allowing your ego to get the best of you.

Conversely, you might also examine if you always take the safe shot. Maybe you are very risk averse in general and should take more risk. There are some risk averse people whose alter ego emerges on the course and throw caution to the wind on the course. That is freeing.

Either way, having a bad lie gives you a chance to think about how you will approach this shot, it's your choice. Will you manage your misses or through caution to the wind? Are you confident or egotistical? Your call – your shot.

❖ ❖ ❖

Hole 7 - Time Management

A round of golf takes between 4 to 4 and a half hours. That's whether you're riding or walking. Like our commuting experiences, sometimes the course gets backed up with traffic. Golf teaches you to manage your time and to be considerate of other people's time. Don't be THAT person who is causing the traffic jam. The golf true lesson is to manage your time so you have fun and ensure that others behind you are also having fun. At the same time, there is an aspect of having compassion for the person slowing you down who may be learning or having a bad round.

If there's no one behind you, you have more time to search for that brand-new ball that is lost in the rough. But if you look behind you and see the foursome behind you standing there aimlessly swinging their clubs while they shoot death stares at you – take that as a signal, to forget the ball, take a drop or let them play through.

There are things your foursome can do if you have fallen behind and want to make up some time. These tips include not making every person hole out on the green, drive a player to their ball and drop them off and go to your ball and get ready to hit, then go pick them up. Play ready golf (make sure everyone agrees first). Let the single guy behind you play through. Only take one practice swing. There are more things you can do but you get the idea.

One of the biggest contributors to delays is once again our friend – Ego. Ego tells you to play from the tips when you can only drive the ball 170 on a good day. Play from the tees that match your skill level. A good rule of thumb is to take your average drive and multiply it by 25 and that will give you the course yardage that fits you. When I was starting out, I made a deal that if I hit the ball double par +2 then I'd pick up the ball so as to not hold others up. So, be flexible and pick up the pace or pick up the ball if others are waiting for you. Be considerate of other's time.

Time management is a great lesson in life, sometimes you can take time and smell the roses and other times you just gotta just speed it up. The real lesson is to be considerate of other's time and to be flexible. You can't hog the course, you can't make the person behind you miss their kid's softball game or dinner with her husband. That's not fair. If you don't like to be rushed, pick a course that is generally not crowded.

At the same time, if you are playing on a holiday weekend (Father's Day) for example, you gotta know that it is going to be a slow round. So just relax and enjoy the moments and count your blessings if you are able to be out with your own father.

❖ ❖ ❖

Hole 8 - Kindness

Have you noticed that there are some people everyone likes to be around? One of the things that makes someone likeable is that they are kind and helpful and are in tune with the feelings of others.

I'm blessed to be married to someone like that. Rich is the person who got me hooked on golf. He reasoned that if I liked to play then it would be something we could do together and ultimately he himself would play more often. Perhaps the initial impetus was more self-interest rather than pure altruism but it worked out for both of us. He's also very smart and understood that if he became my "coach" it wouldn't work very well for our relationship. Pretty much everyone remembers when they were learning to play and what they went through and how someone was kind and patient with them. Kindness on the course is in the simple things, helping someone find their ball, yelling a positive affirmation after someone hit a good shot.

Do people you are playing with watch your drive so that they can help you find your ball? I will confess that sometimes I don't. I will also confess that there are times when I don't watch because I'm busy fussing about my own upcoming drive, washing my ball or getting a new tee out of my bag. I'm working on this.

Opportunities for kindness abound in golf, it might be in asking the single person playing behind you to join you or in giving someone a tip on how to play a hole on the course they've never played before. Offering encouragement or not saying a word when someone is having a tough time and "reading" what you should do is a skill.

I've noticed that when we are kind to others and have good will towards them it seems that everyone plays better. Being generous and kind is allowing the best in us to come out and it reaffirms who we are and makes us feel better. Best of all, it doesn't cost anything to be good to others and will bring a good energy to the round.

❖ ❖ ❖

Hole 9 – If You Can't Laugh At Yourself Don't Worry Others Will

I love to watch Justin Timberlake play golf on TV. I'm a huge fan of his music and he brings the energy and enthusiasm that he shares in his music also to the game of golf. He always has a good time and he is funny, really funny. While he will play the clown on the course, make no mistake, he's a great player. Golf is a game, it's supposed to be fun. Justin embodies the childlike spirit of playing to the game. What is the point of the whole thing if you are so focused on your score that you forget to have a fun?

Games are for kids, and here you have an opportunity to be kid again. My husband plays with a group of pranksters who every year go off and torture each other. Think, exploding golf balls that leave the victim covered in pink dust. They are just silly on the golf course. These middle-aged guys who run businesses and have a lot of responsibility every single day give themselves the gift of being a bunch of goofballs and having fun once a year.

Golf helps you develop a good sense of humor. You have to have a sense of humor because everything will not always go as planned. If you can't laugh at yourself those days when everything seems to go wrong, then one of two things will likely happen, you will be a misery to yourself and those around you, or you will learn to go with the flow and find the humor in the fact that we in fact human after all.

It's the same at work, there's always someone who is complaining; the company sucks, the leaders are a bunch of idiots, the co-workers are all slackers, etc. Hey, it might all be true, but if you can't change it and you really feel that way, then why not just do yourself and everyone else a favor and find something else to do at another company? Somehow, I have a feeling that this type of person would find the same things to complain about at any other company. I know that sounds harsh, but it's not fair to being bringing everyone else down. When you are on the golf course, remind yourself that it is a game, it's supposed to be fun. Take a minute for an attitude adjustment.

If today is an anomaly and you just can't get out of your funk, then at least try to keep your negative thoughts to yourself. Don't pout (yes, I've seen grown men and women pout) and I've done it too, for a hole or two but then I either snap out of it a la Cher in Moonlighting or something happens that brings me back to my happy self. I can't think of a single round that I didn't have fun.

If the first 9 holes were not fun and joyful, then take a minute at the turn and grab an adult beverage or a Gatorade and get ready for the back nine, where redemption awaits.

❖ ❖ ❖

Hole 10 – Resillance

The back nine. You get to fold that scorecard over and you don't have to look at the scores on the front nine again until the end of the round. You have a chance to improve your score and get some great holes in. If you didn't make your hole in one, it can happen on the back nine.

Golf is a game filled with opportunity. Every round, every hole, every shot holds the promise of greatness (or at least, not sucking). There **are** second chances if you can leave the prior shots behind. In the same way that on the first hole you learned about quieting your mind, now you need to leave the front 9 behind, assuming you want the back nine to be better. You get a fresh start on this hole. The mindset of focusing on the present moment applies not only to the round but also to each hole, each shot.

You probably know someone who has been dealt a lousy card in life and remarkably they've found in themselves the strength to be joyful in their day to day lives. I think these people have learned not to be defeated. They have overcome challenges in their lives and have been able to rise above adversity. I bet you can think of someone right now that this applies to.

It takes resolve to come back from a disappointment. I don't know a single person who has called it quits after nine holes because of their poor performance. Golf doesn't give you luxury of being a quitter or sitting this one out on the bench or letting someone else pinch hit. You can't let the opponent win the next match just to get off the court. No, you have to finish the round. You are on the hook and having a lousy attitude is only going to make it worse. So, if the front nine was not your best, you don't have a choice, you have to dig deep and come out swinging. Give yourself a pep talk, you will do better on this hole, you will hit it onto the fairway – your own fairway. You will 1 or 2 putt every hole on the back nine. AND if you can't do that, then put on a happy face and enjoy being out in nature with your friends and have a great time.

    Being able to bounce back and remain positive can make all the difference in a person's life. It will help if you experience a loss of any type, a job, a divorce, a death. Developing this ability early in life is great. Golf is great for kids because they learn exactly this lesson, you can't change the front nine, but you can't quit and you have to dig deep and turn things around so that you and those around you can enjoy the rest of the game.

◆ ◆ ◆

Hole 11 – Better To Lose Your Ball Than Your Temper

I was speaking with a young woman recently about golf and she said she wanted to play more but didn't want to play with her fiancé because he always lost his temper playing golf. Wow, I thought everyone has a bad moment every now and then but all the time seems to be something to work on. Many years ago, my former dentist told me that he got so angry playing golf that he took his brand-new clubs and threw them in a pond and decided never to play again. Seriously? I can't imagine anyone doing something so extreme or having so little self-control over their emotions. Needless to say, I have a new dentist.

Here's something to think about. You hit a bad shot (again) and you're angry with yourself, you explode and your body releases adrenaline. That adrenaline will take between 15 to 20 minutes to flush out of your system. What that means is that the next shot you take will probably also be bad because physically, your body is dealing with tension. Additionally, your focus is not on the shot at hand but replaying negative thoughts. What is gained by that outburst? What should you do instead?

Accept it and focus on the next shot. I play with someone

who when they hit a bad shot, just shrugs and says "oh well" and lets it go. I learned this technique and have incorporated it because it's in the past and you can't change the past. It's not what just happened that counts as much as what you are going to do next. You land in the bunker, "great, this is a chance to practice getting out of the bunker". Visualize where the ball is going to land as it sails out of the bunker.

I learned the hard way not to respond to work emails that are infuriating in the heat of the moment. If I do, I'm more likely to say EXACTLY what I think and that's not going to be productive. It doesn't mean that I don't get angry, just that I'm not going to allow myself to lose control and make things worse.

When someone loses their temper on the course, it makes others very uncomfortable. They don't know what to say. Ultimately, not allowing the anger response to happen, will increase the likelihood that things will improve with the next shot and will make the round more fun for the others around you.

◆ ◆ ◆

Hole 12 – Don't Be An A**Hole

Here's a list of top 10 things that A**holes do on a course. Here's a list of top 10 things that A**holes do on a course.

1. They refuse to be paired up with someone. That's not nice. Sometimes people make assumptions about a person's abilities based on age or gender. They assume they are better. Often, they're wrong. I'm a terrible player and yet, I'm typically not the hold up on the course because I hit straight and don't spend time wandering aimlessly around the course looking for my ball. If we don't encourage younger players to come to love this sport, guess what, you may not have as many courses to play at. My husband and I got paired up with two elderly ladies in Arizona who out-played us in every way. They play every day and kicked our asses. The people you get paired with are 99% of the time, interesting and nice. Enjoy meeting others – don't be rude.

2. They race ahead at the turn and try to go ahead of the people in front of them. Who does that?

3. They are playing slowly and notice the people behind them are faster but refuse to let them play through.

4. They hit into people as "encouragement" to play faster. That's

dangerous. I might know someone who the second time that's happened might have picked up their ball, or run it over with a golf cart or called them out on it. You know who you are.

5. They take 4 practice swings. Geez.

6. They don't fix ball marks on the green and litter the green with sunflower seeds – really???

7. They play from the tips when they shouldn't.

8. They use foul language and show a ton of negative emotion on the course which brings everyone down.

9. They walk across other people's putting line and take an inordinate amount of time measuring every angle of their putting line.

10.   They talk just as you are taking your backswing.

Don't be an A**Hole.

❖ ❖ ❖

Hole 13 – It's Elemental

I love playing in a light rain. It quiets my mind and I decompress. When I play in the rain, I feel proud of myself that I'm out in nature and not letting a few little raindrops stop me from having a good time. Sometimes there is a little mist that rises from the grass that is quite beautiful. The leaves get a deeper shade of green as the grass is satiated with life giving water. It's peaceful.

An unstated but true rule in our co-ed league is that the women will never be the first to will never be ones to suggest that we cancel play. We are tough. That, of course, doesn't mean that we're reckless, if there's a lightning strike and we are called off the course, we comply immediately. Nothing is worth the chance of being hit by lightning, that's just stupid.

While we can't manage the weather, we can manage what we do in response. And here's where being prepared can really be valuable. What's in your golf bag? I keep a light jacket in case it rains and I keep my golf umbrella in the car. My golf bag comes with a cover that will keep my clubs and the grips dry. I typically walk with a push cart and my cart has a place that holds my umbrella in place. Riding in a cart doesn't help much if it rains because the course will be likely be cart path only and you'll end up walking to the ball and getting wet anyway. So just accept it, and recognize that our species is waterproof.

I live in Illinois and will play until there are so many leaves on the course that you can't find the ball. I've brought a blanket for my legs for those early November mornings and have had a shot of Baileys in my coffee to keep me warm. These are happy moments and have an air of survivor to it. If your normal everyday life lacks any real weather challenges, here's a chance to test your mettle.

There is a pretty popular course in our state that has been plagued by gnats. It's a beautiful course where you can sometimes see a bald eagle, but I hate playing there because of the gnats. But I've heard that people continue to play there and put vapor rub on the brim of their visor to deter the gnats from flying in their faces. This is the spirit of golfers that I so admire, that they will find creative ways to not be defeated by the elements.

Oh, and let's not forget the challenges that come with a strong wind. Golfers pinch a few blades of grass, toss it into the air and see how the wind is blowing. I just read that it might be better to look at trees half way between you and your target and observe the direction that the leaves are being blown. The bottom line is that you need to take the conditions into account and make accommodations.

Even sunny days can present challenges. The heat can get you. I've played when it's been extremely hot and then all you can do is try to stay cool by wrapping a cold towel around your neck and making sure you drink a ton of water and Gatorade and watch for danger signs like lack of perspiration.

Every time you play, it won't be 80 degrees and sunny. You can still have a good time but you need to be prepared to align to mother nature's will and find pleasure in being in the elements and sometimes in just knowing that you are tougher than you think.

Hole 14 – For The Ladies

Women make up 19% of golfers. It is a low percentage but it is growing as more and women learn the benefits of golf. I've had the good fortune to play with some remarkable women. They have in their own way inspired me and I have learned lessons from them that have helped me grow as a person.

Younger women may have grown up playing golf and some of us have come to learn how to play later in life. While it has been traditionally hard for women with young children to justify being out of the home for half a day, more and more young mothers are finding ways to squeeze in a quick nine. You need to know that no matter when you start playing, you can learn and even if you take a hiatus, you can come back to the game.

All the material in the other chapters apply to women however, there are special consideration for girls and women. First of all, you have every right to be there. Don't be intimidated by the guys. In fact, golf will teach you to be more confident and assertive. The lessons on the course as you can see here, translate to other areas of your life.

As I said, one of the reasons why women don't play as much as men is because of their family obligations. I want to tell you about a woman I play with who has 4 children. As a young woman, she played as a child and was a caddie. She works full time in corporate America and takes care of her family who have their own activities that she has to take them to. Yet, somehow, she has prioritized squeezing out a few hours each week to play 9 holes in a weeknight league – two hours. This woman has played while pregnant up until her 9th month. I don't advise you to do this without a doctor's o.k. but it goes to show that if you are fit you can do it. The point is that those few hours are a luxury and a respite from all the other obligations that she has in her life. This is time for her and it is more active and fun than getting a mani/pedi. She is doing something that she enjoys that helps to balance the other demands on her busy life.

    If you are blessed to be married, you may find that an advantage to golf is being able to play with your husband. If you both like to play, then you will share experiences like planning vacations to play dreamed of courses. There are so many beautiful courses in far-away places. These experiences stand out in my mind as much as any sightseeing tour.

    I used to think that men resented seeing women on the course, I don't feel that way anymore. Either they have gotten used to us or it was never really true and just something in my own head. Bottom line, you belong there, we all have a place.

    And golf clothes are sooooo cute. Enjoy!

❖ ❖ ❖

Hole 15 – Aging And Limitations

It's not fun when you can't do something you want to do because of a physical limitation and that can happen at any age.

Tiger Woods just won the Masters for the 5th time. He is a legend and an incredible athlete. A lot of folks thought he was pretty much through given all the physical issues he's had which included the following: .

December 1994: Knee Surgery
Dec. 13, 2002: Second knee surgery
August 2007: Ruptured ACL but keeps playing and wins 5 out of 6 tournaments
April 15, 2008: Has third knee surgery
May 2008: two stress fractures of the left tibia
June 24, 2008 fourth knee surgery,
December 2008: Injures the Achilles tendon in his right leg
March 31, 2014: First back surgery for a pinched nerve.
Sept. 16, 2015: Second back surgery
October 2015: Third back surgery
April 20, 2017: Undergoes a fourth back surgery – a spinal fusion

So pretty much two years after spinal fusion, he comes back and wins the Masters. Can you imagine what it must have been like to be Tiger Woods? To be at the top and have set back after set back because of physical injuries and to have to work hard to come back? I honestly can't imagine how difficult it must have been for Tiger Woods during his recovery period. But he got through it.

Look, we're all aging and with we will lose flexibility and might have to start doing things a little differently. I recently saw a great golf tip for seniors which was to place your rear foot a little bit behind your front foot, which helps provide greater range of motion. The truth is that seniors do play and they have more spare time in retirement to play. I hope to play well into my old age because it will help keep me young and will give me a chance to socialize and meet new people.

I recently played with a man who was in his 80's and his son. What a joy to see this man playing and having a great time. Getting out there will keep you young and vibrant.

◆ ◆ ◆

Hole 16 – Parenting

More and more, I see parents and their children at the practice range and out on the course. It warms my heart to see them out there because I know they are teaching their children a game that will set them up to grow in so many ways. They will learn resilience, dedication and good sportsmanship. Some of these young people will be leaders in their schools and later in business, government and churches. It's great that they are learning these important skills and lessons while they are young.

They day comes when these young people become teenagers. What a blessing in these days of texting and gaming for these young people to have an opportunity to unplug for a few hours and to get some sunshine in a safe place. Teens are notorious for not wanting to be seen with their parents. But because golf has fewer opportunities for being seen in public by their friends, it is a way to still connect and spend time with parents at this crucial point in their lives.

What a blessing for teenagers to disconnect from the barrage of texts and incredible school workload that most face. Golf gives them, like us, a way to be free from all the worries and anxieties of their hectic lives.

I have the good fortune to sometimes play with one of our children, Mark. Mark is now a grown man practicing law in Chicago. His life is crazy busy and playing together gives us a chance to catch up in a fun way doing something we both enjoy.

I would encourage parents to start their children off at a young age and to use all that this great game has to offer to teach them resiliency, honesty, dedication, hard work, compassion, and to approach life with a spirit of joy and fun.

❖ ❖ ❖

Hole 17 – Wild Wildlife

I recently had one of the most breathtaking experiences of my life that I want to share with you. We were playing at a resort in upper Michigan, pretty far out there. We had been told that there was there was an Eagle's nest on the course and of course, we had no trouble finding it because we could hear the eaglets calling for their parents to bring them food. In retrospect, maybe we took maybe a little too long admiring the babies. We got on that hole's elevated green and looked up and saw the mother eagle coming straight at us. AHHHHH. She was enormous and then proceeded to fly low around us, making a circle around us before flying back to the nest. Clearly, she was warning us to stay away from the babies. It was magnificent. She was the so beautiful and it was awe inspiring to see this majestic symbol of our American freedom so close to us. I'll never forget it.

Most of us don't get a chance to see wild animals too often in our daily lives yet I have seen the following on golf courses: coyote, frogs, toads, cranes, herons, snakes, rabbits, scorpions, alligators, hawks, deer, a multitude of smaller birds, roadrunners, an owl and a bald eagle and her eaglets. Each encounter is a surprise and instills a respect for nature. Maybe because I was raised in a city, I find the ability to experience nature directly so awe inspiring.

The fact that I can see all this on display while I'm playing golf is another benefit. I sometimes wonder, if we didn't play golf and the course didn't exist what would happen to the ecosystem that is peaceful co-existing with us here. Certainly, it would not take long for houses and stores to be put up and for these animals to be displaced and die. While it might seem overly sentimental, it is a reality that we have decreased the amount of open green land in most states. The game that I love allows for nature to exist in our midst. It truly is a rare privilege and another reason to love all the opportunities that this game provides and to share it with others.

◆ ◆ ◆

Hole 18 – Gratitude

Golf is an expensive sport. It's a sport that is still somewhat for the wealthier among us. I was born very poor, a first generation Cuban American. When my parents brought me home from the hospital in New Jersey, it was to a small apartment that had no running hot water. It is a testament to our great country and to God that my life has unfolded in the way that it has, and that I have the means to play this great game. Growing up, the closest large park was 10 minutes away by car, meaning it was difficult to play sports that took a lot of space like tennis, golf was non-existent. Every day of my life, I am grateful for all the opportunities I've been given to work hard and achieve my goals. I am aware that everyone doesn't get those breaks in life.

So, yes, we should be grateful that we can play golf, even that we have golf clubs at all are really something to marvel at. Think about the design and work that has gone into those clubs. Maybe you inherited clubs from a parent or a friend, be grateful that you can continue to use them.

Be grateful that you have the physical ability to play. Not everyone who wants to play golf can continue to play. Gratitude is a beautiful thing, be grateful for your friends, the beautiful day, the fact that you are surrounded by mature trees and for the animals that share the land with you today.

Be grateful for the young people taking up this game who will preserve this game and the land it is played on.

You fought your way through your own self-doubts, you controlled your temper, you helped your fellow man or woman, you played through the rain and enjoyed it, you hit your farthest drive, you only 3 putted on two holes and you had fun today with your friends. Well done.

Now as you get onto the 18th hole, before your set up, pause for a moment and take it all in, the beautiful clubhouse that awaits you. This will be the best hole yet. Whether it has been a great round or a challenge, you have made it and now it is time to finish strong. See you at the 19th hole.

◆ ◆ ◆

The 19Th Hole – Camaraderie

We finished our round and now we can sit back and enjoy a cool iced tea or another beverage of choice. We have a chance to reflect with our friends on the good holes we had and have a few laughs. We can plan for the next outing and tell each other about the other courses we have played. As a golfer you are part of this group, you are one of the lucky people who have the physical and financial ability to play. There are a couple of courses that I play at which I frequently see older retired gentlemen playing cards after the round. Friendships are formed through shared experiences. Our friends are people who we have shared time with us in one way or another. Our golf friendships are special, we look forward to seeing our friends and catching up on what is happening with them. We look forward to the next time we can get out there and play again.

I hope, dear friend that you have enjoyed playing a round with me today. I hope this small book has given you some things to think about and that you will continue to play and encourage others to take up the game, especially the young. © 2019, Marilyn Merrifield, all rights reserved

Made in the USA
Monee, IL
25 September 2023